MW01243359

GRANDMA THE SEX POT

by

ADELAIDE JACOBS-SIEGEL

authorHOUSE®

AuthorHouse™
1663 Liberty Drive, Suite 200
Bloomington, IN 47403
www.authorhouse.com
Phone: 1-800-839-8640

The names of the people in my book are fictitious or deceased. Also, my memory in not 100% accurate after all these years.

First published by AuthorHouse 11/8/2007

ISBN: 978-1-4343-3441-1 (sc)

Printed in the United States of America
Bloomington, Indiana

This book is printed on acid-free paper.

Introduction

I soon learned that the male ego and the woman's cunt were the most powerful things in the world".

A wise man once said, "You don't know men until you've had a hundred men, happy to say". After my divorce, I met my quota.

Remember sex is wonderful if you enjoy it and no one gets hurt".

Men think with their bottom head, women think with their top head   …………..they usually arrive at the same place.

I guess sex is here to stay.

So let's get on with the stories of my wonderful sex life. I'm 85 years old and still enjoy having some good sex.

Chapter 1

I was born into a comfortable family in the 20th century in Cleveland, Ohio. We always had help in the house and my parents were very social. They were always going out to fancy parties and having friends over. My only sister was born 14 months after me. Someone told my mother that she couldn't become pregnant while nursing me. Over the years my sister was spanked frequently and I became Miss Goody Goody. She had a quite temper, she pulled a knife on me during an argument one time. I was always my fathers favorite and she resented me for that. My parents divorced in my late teens. That's when I realized how selfish my mother was. We lived in a 3 bedroom house with my grandmother at the time. My mother made my sister and I sleep in the same bed, a twin bed at that, while she slept in the master bedroom on a double bed. Of course grandma had her own room.

My sister was thin and I was a bit heavy. I lost weight when I started to menstruate at the age of 12. By the time I was 15, I had a steady boyfriend, Manny. We necked but that was all. He was also a virgin and said he would stay that way till we got married. He always brought me candy, cigarettes, a wristwatch and other nice gifts. When I was 18, I met another fellow, Herb, and dated him also. Both Manny and Herb wanted to give me engagement rings for my 18th birthday, but my mother said no. She didn't like Manny's mother and said Herb didn't have a good enough job to support me so she sent me to my Aunt Lil's house in Mansfield, Ohio, about 75 miles away. There I met my husband-to-be Arthur, at a picnic in Mt. Vernon, Ohio. He managed a small town department store, a chain outfit, in Marion, Ohio. In the fall, I went to Ohio State University, which was in Columbus, Ohio, 50 miles from Marion. Arthur came to visit me every Sunday and also came home with me to meet my parents. My whole family adored him and we became engaged as soon a school was out. We married the following February. Art, as I called him was 25 and I was 19 when we married. Art was quiet, he said "better to be thought a fool than to open your mouth and confirm it". He had a big hind end and used to say "you can't drive a nail with a tack hammer".

I had done some heavy necking, but was still a virgin, and to be honest I was a little afraid of sex. On my wedding night I bled, which I knew I should, but every time he entered me, I bled for three months. I went to the doctor who said I was "not open yet", but that I had broken an artery. He fixed me up then my husband and I started to have more sex. My husband would come, but I never did, so I would masturbate when I felt like it. After 5 years of unsatisfying sex, I read in a magazine, that I was supposed to come too and told my husband. That's when we really started having sex, enjoyable sex. My husband had a large penis and if he waited long enough, I came too.

My husband quit the chain store and we went into our own ready to wear business. I worked 12 hours a day in the store and we prospered. After three years, I became pregnant and worked up until I was nine months, then I quit. Shortly after my parents divorce my mother sold her house and moved in with me and Art, she started working in our store too. After the war, my husband opened a children's store and my mother ran it. She lived with us for 15 years till I finally married her off to a wealthy jeweler. Meanwhile, I worked in the store for holidays and ran a sample sale of coats and suits in my basement. I also moved my in-laws from New York to Cleveland. We bought a house for them. They were originally from Germany and spoke very little English. Meanwhile I was busy being a wife, mother, daughter, sister, daughter-in-law, and also managed to maintain a social life with a swimming club that we belonged to. My husband and I had 3 children in all, 2 girls and 1 boy.

I became an excellent cook, but never learned how to do housework. I always had help in the house, but I did the cooking at which I was excellent. I kept moving and redoing houses until we had a lovely large new home. I made a lot of money that way. My husband worked every night till 9 o'clock and by the time he came home it was late. Sometimes I would surprise him wearing just a fur piece or a big black scarf, a fox stole or a black nightgown. I asked him if he was ever bored with me and he said, "No, I never know what to expect". When I came near him he would often put his hands across his chest. He later explained that he got hot and bothered and didn't want the children to see.

Art was satisfied with our lives, but I wasn't. I started to want more, so I went to a therapist and my husband did too. He had trouble showing his love expect with gifts on holidays. I needed more so I went to a divorce lawyer. My uncle was my husband's lawyer and didn't believe in divorce. They tried to starve my young daughter and me into conciliation, but my lawyer said to sell anything I wanted to in the house, for food and money for my daughter and me. I had beautiful dresses, German beer mugs, knick knacks and other valuable, which I sold. At the time of my divorce, I was 47 years old. After my divorce I went to Florida to the Harbor Island Spa where the best part of my life began. I became a real woman. I learned about sex, men, and life outside of family. My lawyer wanted to have an affair but I said no. I waited until I moved to Florida.

Chapter 2

History

I entered the school of pleasure as a freshman and graduated magna cum laude and became "Grandma the Sexpot". After loosing 20 pounds, going from size 16 to 12, I went down to the Harbor Island Spa in Florida to see my daughter and 2 year old grandson and to tone up with the massages. I was 36B, 28-inch waist, 34 inch hips, and had long lovely legs.

After dinner the second night, a tall well built gentleman, who sat at the next table, asked if he could join me for coffee. He had a certain confidence about him. Of course, I said yes. After 10 minutes conversation, I said, I don't go to bed. He said he was patient. A year and a half later, when my divorce was final I returned to the spa, where I met him and began a torrid love affair. His name was Harry and he was quite a man, a graduate pharmacist, but didn't like that profession so he gave it up to become a theatrical agent. He played a fantastic piano and wrote "Uncle Miltie's" material when he was Mr. Texaco. He was well acquainted with a lot of stars at the time. He retired here after a long illness. He was a sharp dresser; he had his shirts custom-made with wide collars and wore imported sweaters on occasion. He smoked big Havana cigars and really made a good appearance. He had an air that showed he knew his way around any person or situation. He played piano a couple nights at hotels on the beach and also wrote some material for local talent. He was a fantastic lover and taught me a great deal about making love, dressing, hairstyles, and makeup. He was just what I needed after the divorce. In bed he was the greatest. He taught me how to enjoy lovemaking from sucking, fucking, and teaching me about the 69 Japanese ways to enjoy sex.

Harry was 7½ years older than me but was young at heart. The first time we had sex at the spa, we both undressed and got into bed. He kissed me, his tongue exploring my whole mouth, then he moved down to my breasts which he kissed and sucked, first one then the other. Then he slowly moved his mouth down to my cunt which he licked, and drove me wild. At last, he entered me with his dark, beautiful penis and we both came together. We rested for a half hour and then had a repeat performance. It was heavenly. I felt like a bride on her wedding night. After several nights of this, he taught me to lick his balls and kiss them. He also had a glass of champagne which he told me to dip his penis into and lick it off. It was exciting and thrilling for both of us. Instead of bridge and golf, I took to sucking and fucking.

Harry made love to every part of my body and life was beautiful. He helped me settle into my new apartment, found a doctor and dentist for me. Any little thing I needed, he was there for me. He taught me how to do my hair and makeup, I was often called "The White Owl" girl. I had good taste in clothes but he showed me sexier styles, like gold snake shoes, pink shoes, and clothes that flattered my figure. He introduced me to show business. I met many theatrical people and we enjoyed life together. We went to Key West one weekend and he introduced me to conch and the flavor of the Keys. It was wonderful there.

The water on both sides had a flavor all their own. After a few months, I decided to take a real estate course at night as I wanted to be with my young daughter during the day. She was fourteen at the time. After the 6-month course, which I passed, as well as the state exam, I went to work for a land company. I worked four hours a day on Lincoln Road and learned to sell the American dream, a piece of land for a home. Of course, the land companies at that time were not really legitimate. I hesitated to do this, but I figured if I didn't someone else would. The pay was good and it left me time for my daughter and my boyfriend. I went from a suburban housewife to the real world of looking out for number one, me. We were together every day or night or both. He was friendly with a former singer he had managed who now worked at Sak's and her boyfriend who was the former vice-president of Lily of France bras. She was quite a beautiful women. She went to Paris every year to model for the bra show. After her first marriage to a wealthy man who abused her, she divorced him and became a lesbian. But I guess only on a part time basis because interestingly enough she still liked men. She dressed very sexy all the time. She even wore beautiful undergarments in the pool as bathing suits. On her they looked good. We doubled dated with her and her boyfriend but I was afraid to be alone with her. She still liked women, and I wasn't into women.

Harry had some other friends, two sisters who owned a small hotel off the beach, which several actors visited. They also owned a small six unit apartment house. Their father visited every night and he had a routine of going down on the elderly female tenants to keep them happy, in order to collect rents. Harry also sent me to Nassau with two of the sharp women from my real estate office to learn some things, nothing about business though. They taught me things such as picking up men to pay for dinner and buy us our quota of liquor the next day. I never knew these things from my life in Cleveland. I was really a hick but caught on fast and somehow I attracted the men for the two girls and myself. I guess my innocence was attractive to them. I was a slow starter but a fast learner.

At the spa, both times I was there, a wealthy pork dealer from Boston was there too. He took me to some shows, after Harry said okay, and told me how to pass the time but I wouldn't go to bed with them. I told him I had an infection that he wouldn't want to give his wife. He called me from Boston several times and finally asked me to meet him in Chicago where he was going to sell his meat plant for 10 million dollars. I had another boyfriend in Chicago, Joe, who used to call me to have an affair with him when I was married. I always said no of course because I was married. I figured I might as well take the trip, kill two birds with one stone. My first night in Chicago was spent with Mr. pork dealer, we went to a lovely restaurant and had a good time. I didn't like him though, he was short and just not my type.

The second day in Chicago I called Joe, he told me to go to a local hotel, register, and he would meet me later, which he did. He was a stunning tall handsome man, six foot two with the smallest penis I ever saw. He had three children though so I guess size doesn't matter. He came to the hotel around 6 o'clock and we went to bed right away. We fooled around for about an hour but he couldn't "get it up". He blamed it on the anticipation of waiting 20 years to have me. So, we got dressed and went to the Playboy Club for dinner figuring we would finish up later. After dinner and the show we went back to the hotel and the red light was flashing on the telephone. It was a call from Cleveland. My mother was in the hospital. Joe made arrangements for me to get a plane out in the morning and he took me to the airport. So, we never consummated our affair.

After I came back, Harry went to New York to visit his daughter for two weeks. He left me a plastic dildo to use if I got horny. Instead I went shopping. I needed some shoes and went to a shoe store in Surfside. The manager was a young man seven years younger than me from Columbus, Ohio and we got friendly. He asked me for a date and I said, "yes". Youth is interesting, going to watch the planes, having sex on the floor, watching television, interesting meals and of course, lots of new shoes for me. I had bought two pairs of shoes at the store and he bought me another four pairs that I looked at. He was a nice youthful looking man. When Harry came back, he was angry and accused me of robbing the cradle, since the young man was seven years younger than I was. He upset me so much that I called my therapist in Cleveland, he assured me it was all right.

Chapter 3

Fred

I had a good stockbroker, an interesting young man with a wealthy father and rich wife. He thought I was very sexy and suggested I open a country club for private customers. I wasn't interested but he promised to be my very best customer and that he would also send me customers. I never had sex with him, although he wanted to, but he kissed me once and came in his pants. Needless to say, I never went into business.

Almost every night after the shows, Harry and I went to the Concorde Cafeteria where entertainers and interesting people hung out. The talk there was about different acts and different lines the actors used. Hmmm interesting.

I started to go to a beauty shop on 41st Street and after a while I heard the girls talking about a madam they worked for at night who had many wealthy clients from South America. They were making a fortune in money and jewels. I learned about "daisy chains", a circle of men and women sucking and fucking. They also had small ice cubes in their mouth when they were sucking a man's penis, which was supposed to give them added thrill. They asked me to join them.

The money was excellent but while I was thinking about joining them, the madam got arrested and that was that. I never mentioned it to Harry. Meanwhile, I was learning a lot about show business. It prepared me for a future job as a social director at some of the hotels. After year or so, my daughter decided to move north to live with her father. She didn't like the schools in Florida.

I had my boyfriend and two of his friends over for the holidays. One being the vice president of Lily of France bras, the other a local artist, we had a lovely time. I was a good cook and they each brought a bottle of liquor. During dinner, my landlord knocked on my door and told me I left some burns on the carpeting when I moved from my old two-bedroom apartment to a one-bedroom apartment after my daughter moved out. I excused myself and went next door to see the burns. When we were in the apartment, Fred, my landlord grabbed me and kissed me. I was shocked. He told me that he had gotten a divorce and had always been interested in me. I told him I had to get back to my guests but would speak with him tomorrow. I invited him and his son to join us for dessert. Believe it or not I still got surprised when a man made a pass at me. After dinner, the four men and I went upstairs to a neighbor's apartment. She wanted the artist to look over her husband's pictures. We then went to sit outside at the pool, which was on Biscayne Bay and was very beautiful at night. I made quite a sight, with four men following me all around the building.

I was also friendly with some neighbor's who came to this country from Jamaica, Pauline and her husband with their 18 year old son and 20 year old daughter. Pauline had a brother who had been the head of a Jamaican government and another brother who was the Prime Minister to England. When her mother visited, she enjoyed hearing about me and all my boyfriends. She was quite the matriarch. Pauline and her husband traveled a lot, trying to get their money out their country. At that time it was very hard. Harry and I took Pauline's son and daughter to dinner, Jai-Alai, football games and many other outings. I became very close with her children. Her daughter became pregnant by her married cousin. She had an abortion and confided in me. Her parents never knew. Pauline invited me for Jamaican dishes and I invited them back for American food. Her husband loved my homemade chicken soup and lemon pies. Over the years she remained my one good girlfriend in Florida.

The next day my landlord called and asked if I needed any groceries, as he was going shopping. I said yes and he picked me up. We went food shopping. He talked to strangers, asking if they needed an apartment, he had two vacant in his building. When we returned home, my boyfriend Harry was waiting in the lobby. I forgot I was supposed to go someplace with him. Fred, who paid for my groceries, told my boyfriend he was going to have a good dinner. And that's when the trouble started between Harry and me.

My landlord's ex-wife was cheating on him with their son's singing teacher and he caught them. He went to Mexico to get a divorce. Harry said that the music teacher was going down on his wife, eating her and she liked it. She on the other hand told Fred he was no good in bed and emotionally castrated him, at least temporarily until I got him going. Anyhow, my boyfriend was angry with me for spending so much time with Fred, so we weren't as close. I figured, why not have a little fun with Fred, teaching him all the things Harry had taught me about me sex. And when he caught on we started having amazing sex.

Fred started calling me a lot even when he was in New York. He owned two 50-unit apartment buildings with his brothers on Nassau Street, a jewelry store filled building. The next time he came to Florida he called and wanted to see me. But I said I didn't want the tenants to know because they would start bothering me when they needed something. I didn't want that. We tried going out to unusual places to avoid being seen but still managed to bump into tenants from my building. And just as I suspected, they starting harassing me, I just told them to talk to Fred. It was pretty annoying but, Fred was very generous with gifts and trips, so I let it pass.

Fred was tall and had a youthful look about him. He was three months older than me. He was well built like an athlete, with golden brown hair and blue eyes. He was almost like an overgrown kid and very enthusiastic about life. He enjoyed almost everything, golf, shopping and life in general. He treated me like a new found toy.

Now the tables had turned, I was the teacher not the student and Fred turned out to be an excellent student. He was very anxious to learn. He knew the basics but had to learn to enjoy each step more: longer kisses, making love to the whole body and experimenting with different ways to give and receive pleasure. Basically, he had to learn how to fuck. He was like a kid, ready to come right away. I had to slow him down. When we made love the first time he had a hard time getting it up. I gently talked to him and his penis about how wonderful they both were and slowly his penis sprung into action. Once he was over the hump he became quite good in bed. He wasn't as big as Harry or my first husband, but he was adequate. I didn't know they came in sizes.

Fred and I traveled a lot and he was always very generous towards me with clothes, jewels, and extravagant outings. He even sent my young daughter a pearl ring for Christmas at my request. We went to the Catskills and Nassau often, also Freeport, Jamaica and many other tropical locales. When I was with him in New York we saw plays and went shopping. We enjoyed being together. Meanwhile, Harry, who was still in the picture, was very jealous and angry with me. He taunted me by saying Fred would never marry me. I guess he thought that would bother me. Little did he know I didn't want to get married to anyone, including Fred, I was too busy enjoying life.

I decided to ask for a transfer from my job in the land business to an out of town location. I was offered a position in Busch Gardens, Tampa or Ocala. I took Ocala. It was a small town but land sales were booming there. I moved into a hotel that had a hotplate and a small refrigerator that I could keeps snacks in. Fred visited me often and I went back Miami every other weekend. Things were going good between us. Eventually Harry and I broke up. Not too long after that, I ended up moving back to Miami. Ocala was just not for me, I was used to a faster pace of living. Plus my new boss was trying to get into my pants.

It was Christmas time and my daughter was visiting, Fred's family was also in town visiting him. Fred and I were feeling really horny but my daughter was in my apartment and his son and brother were in his and all the hotel rooms in town were booked. We could've done it in the car but we didn't want to get caught. So Fred said that he had a vacant apartment that he had just put new carpeting in and asked if I would go there. I said yes and we had a quite a roll on the carpet. We had many interesting and exciting experiences. One time when we were in the Catskills we met a nice couple that thought I was Mrs. Schecter, Fred's wife. Two months later we went to Nassau with another couple Fred knew. I ran into some old friends who asked for my husband. It seemed everyone assumed we were married. Fred's son also went on this trip, so I had my own room. Fred and I would have to sneak in a fuck every now and then. Another couple asked for my husband and I had to guide them away from his son and explain that we weren't married.

When I was alone in Florida, I played bridge and joined the Cabana Club at the Fontainebleau with some single women from my building. At the bridge club, I met an Englishman, Captain Arthur Clegg, who owned a yacht next to the Playboy Club. We played bridge and I went out on the yacht with him quite often. Other women ran after him, but I didn't, so he wanted to marry me. Of course I said no. He was a world traveler, born in England, and was a citizen of Canada, fantastic at bridge, dancing, but not the greatest lover. He was alright to pass the time with, but still enjoyed Fred, my landlord too.

Fred asked me to live with him in New York on a trial basis for marriage. I said no, I wasn't interested in getting married again, twenty-eight years was enough. Fred didn't like being alone and I wouldn't consider marrying him, or anyone else, so we broke up.

Fred gave me some pretty jewelry and we had many good memories. He even loaned me some money in New York after we broke up. Many years later, he called me in Florida, he was remarried but wanted to see me. We went for dinner and roll in the hay. Fond memories.

Chapter 4

One day I went to the Fontainebleau Cabana Club with a girl from my building. She left me alone at the pool and some gentleman introduced himself to me. His name was David. He asked me for a dinner date that night and I said I would let him know later. My friend returned and I told her about him. She said he was the eccentric millionaire that everyone talked about. He played scrabble at the Cabana Club every day. I told him I would join him dinner. He picked me up at home around 6 o'clock with an interesting car, a T-bird, a 16-year old classic with a hard canvas top. We went to a fancy restaurant and all the valet parking attendants went wild over it. Everyone seemed to know him at the restaurant and some people even sent us drinks. David was tall and slim with broad shoulders. He reeked of sex. Being near him, you felt sexy.

When we arrived home, he kissed me goodnight and wanted to come in and get friendlier. I said no, he responded "I know, my mother, my sister and you are all virgins" and left. I felt badly but that was that. The next day at the pool he apologized and asked me out for dinner again. After dinner we went to his place. He wanted to show me his apartment, besides I had previously said that I never had sex in my apartment because my daughter lived with me. He had a charming apartment and before I knew it he had me in bed. He was built well and sex was good. After I started seeing him, I would get undressed and put on his shirts, and tied it at my pussy, which fascinated him.

We talked a lot and he was surprised that he could talk to a woman, since he thought they were only for sex.

Of course, David knew all the right moves and I enjoyed all my experiences with him and his friends. He was never married and had no children. His whole life was devoted to pleasuring himself and whoever was with him. I had many interesting experiences with him. Several times we went to burlesque shows. Sometimes the audience was hotter than the stage. I saw one woman raise her sweater and play with her nipples and look real happy. Another man was playing with his penis and jerked himself off. Some couples were feeling each other up. The shows were always about the same thing, strippers and comedians. It was okay to go once in a while.

David had a car wash up North, which his brother ran for him. He paid him a good salary and all he could steal. He didn't mind because his brother had two children to raise. He told me about a teacher he had dated, who liked him to pee on her after sex. He went to Grossinger's in the Catskills every summer and traveled to England to shop for his slacks. He had a good friend in the next apartment that joined us for dinner sometimes. One night after dinner, David asked me to have sex with his friend. I said yes as it was exciting doing it with his friend while he watched. Then after his friend left I had sex with him. Quite a night. The next morning, he made me Nova lox, bagels and coffee. He always had a refrigerator full of goodies. He was learning to cook and keep his apartment clean. I supervised some of his efforts and he soon learned. Life was good...good food, good sex.

One time, David had a nice young couple over to have sex with me. The man was a young, tall blonde with a huge penis and his girlfriend was a sweet young girl. She sucked my breasts and my vagina after he came into me. It was very interesting and good but I wouldn't make a habit of it. I just liked to try new things as he thought of them. On another occasion, David wanted to go to a hotel where couples went to meet other couples to have sex with. I didn't want to go and he said he wouldn't force me if I didn't want to go. We ended up going and several different couples wanted to join us, but I said no and David took me home.

David was obviously very adventurous when it came to sex. One night he wanted to have sex with his penis in my ass. I agreed to try it but only if he was gentle. It was good but I was afraid to do it again because I had hemorrhoids. Try anything once.... ALMOST!

Often David would have friends in from the north and they joined us for dinner. I used to ask him if dinner was formal. If he said yes, I wore my false eyelashes, otherwise I didn't.

We joined some friends at the Fontainebleau, a couple of men and several young girls. One of the men was an actor from the Dean Martin Show. He asked me for a date for the next day. I was flattered but I said no, I was busy.

One time David had a friend from the north coming for dinner. When I arrived before his guest, he was naked and me to undress. When his friend came he sent out to get Kentucky fried chicken for all of us. When he returned, he undressed and we all had dinner on David's living room floor. David made drinks and we had a good time. David and his friend touched me occasionally, then David asked me to go to bed with his friend, so I did. We all had fun. His friend was married but not happily so I made him happy for one night. David bought me a radio for being so nice to his friend.

One time he had a couple of sister prostitutes over. He invited me but I didn't go. He watched them have sex and then he had them. He wanted to try everything in life. I didn't. Some yes, some no. So I started breaking things off with David gradually. My friend Claire was over and the doorbell rang. It was David, he came in and had a drink.

He told Claire that I was trying to get rid of him and that he would never let me go. On the way out he touched Claire's breast and I thought she would die. I was past being shocked by him. I really outgrew him and was ready for others. He was written up in Bessie Grossinger's book. He was really interesting.... in rare ways.

Some time before breaking things off with David, I saw an ad for a four unit apartment complex in Bay Harbor, a nice neighborhood. I bought it for $70,000. My stockbroker recommended an attorney who helped me get a loan. The attorney owned a nudist camp and invited me. I said no because I was two-toned. Blonde on my head and brunette on my pussy. I bought the apartment complex and made friends with the owners there after six months. One of the tenants was moving out so I decided to sell the building instead of looking for a new tenant. I put an ad in the paper and had quite a few customers. I always advertised *cream puff* for sale. A young man named Ben, in the moving business, said he wanted to buy my building and I agreed to hold it for him for a week so he could get financing. He gave me a thousand-dollar deposit. He came over with friends or by himself, but never with his wife. One night he came over and picked me up. I asked, "what are you doing"? He said "taking you to bed". I said, "No, not until I get the 10% down".

Ben bought the building that gave me a $20,000 profit in six months. Not bad. Anyhow we finally went to bed. Ben was 15 years younger than me but good sex doesn't know age. His wife was busy with the children, school and everything else, so I enjoyed talking with him as well as the sex. He was good in bed but liked it doggie fashion. That was okay because I would try anything. We became good friends and carried on a wonderful affair which lasted almost twenty years.

Ben was in the moving business and he moved me many times. No charge, of course. I bought another 6-unit building, this time for $98,000 and moved into that one. Ben moved me and I became good friends with his wife and two children. His wife was a teacher and a lousy cook. So I would go over there and cook for them sometimes. Potato pancakes, turkeys etc. Ben said he couldn't continue going to bed with me because of my friendship with his family. After a week or so, he changed his mind and continued to come over, calling first and always bringing me dinner. He was a good friend and lover and helped when necessary with the building.

The 6-unit building I bought had one two bedroom and five single room apartments, all furnished. Different apartment owners in the neighborhood were very friendly and helpful, especially a man named Harry. Looks like I'm a magnet for guys named Harry. He wasn't too tall, about two inches taller than me. He was very pleasant and would give you the shirt off his back. He had a tree removed for me and never let me pay. He was too good-hearted: he lost a lot of money that way. He was a widower with one daughter who had a big home on the Island in Bay Harbor. She was known as "The Rose Lady" as she grew beautiful roses. He bought me a mixer and would come over to make whiskey sours some afternoons.

If he was busy helping different people he would call me "doll" (he said I was a doll).

Harry had a girlfriend who was a nurse in the area. I started dating him sometimes because she worked the night shift and slept during the day. He took me to fine restaurants and we always had a good time. When he took me to bed, he was a jackrabbit. I slowed him down to a slower pace and he really started to enjoy sex. I actually helped his penis grow by teaching him to slow down. I told my doctor about it at my next visit, he jumped up and unzipped his fly, pulled out his penis and said, "Look what you did to me"! I ran out of the office and needless to say, I never returned to that doctor's office again.

Harry was pleasant looking and very sweet. He brought me lox, bagels, cream cheese, smoked fish and Napoleons every Sunday as he did his girlfriend and daughter who had a big house on in Bay Harbor. When she wasn't home I went over there with Harry and went swimming in the nude. It was lovely.

My best girlfriend at the time Sandy, her husband Bernie and she owned two apartment buildings that her father bought for them. On a trip to Florida with her two children, they were so worn out that her father came down and bought them these 2 buildings. One was 12 units the other 4. The smartest thing

Sandy's husband ever did was marry her. He was good looking and there were rumors of him going to single men's apartments and sitting around in the nude. Rumors, rumors, rumors. Sandy fixed me up with one of Bernie's visiting cousins. He was a big handsome fellow, younger than me. He picked me up for dinner at the dog track where we went every night for dinner and the races. He was a heavy bettor. I bet a couple of times but gave up because it was too hard to pick winners. He usually lost every night but only twice in the two weeks he was visiting. Those nights he was so happy he wanted to sleep with me. It was alright with me as he was good-looking and knew the right moves. He was OK in bed but I'd had better. I just helped him enjoy his vacation.

Someone introduced me to a new widower, a nice man about 60. He picked me up every Saturday at noon to go to the track to see the races. He bought me lunch and did some betting. He told me how much he missed his wife, who used to go to the track with him every Saturday and he was grateful for my company. After a month of Saturdays I made some excuse and quit going with him. I guess I helped him through the loss of his wife but he was a dead end for me. He was my height and had no personality. Definitely not my type. He never made a pass at me. He just wanted my company.

An English friend of mine, Arthur, and different men in the neighborhood helped me when things needed fixing in my building. Arthur was well built, with a mustache and he was very British looking. His penis was rather small but sex wasn't the most important thing in our relationship. Bridge and dancing (which I loved) were.

I came to Florida with stocks and cash worth around $75,000. Between stock dividends, the market, and my buildings I worked sometimes, between the land company which was four hour shifts and as a social director at different hotels. I managed to do many different things. The first hotel I worked at was the Carillon. I learned the business there, from dance parties, egg toss, which got Grace Kelley's brother and friends attention who where deciding where to have the Olympics. They enjoyed the egg toss, pie eating contest and many activities. I didn't date when I worked there. I worked a split shift, 10 to l pm then 6-10pm. During the time that I was social directing at a hotel on 69th street, Sandy asked me to fix her aunt up. I said "okay". I asked one of the single men at the hotel to meet her. He agreed but wanted me to go along. I said no, but he wanted to fix me up with a wealthy man from the hotel, who had the penthouse suite. I said "alright". We all met and Sandy's aunt up and the man I fixed up with hit it off and they began dating. The man I was fixed up with fell for me and wanted to see me whenever he could. He took me shopping and introduced me to several of his friends and his family, where we had dinner one night. I went with him to get a suit he ordered, it didn't fit right and I made the store sell him on that did. He was glad that I handled things for him. He asked me to marry him and surprisingly I said "yes". We went to a spa for a week but he was so jealous all the time that I broke up with him. Money wasn't everything. I was right, single was better. The Sandy fixed me up with an uncle of hers. We went to a movie and after there was a ladies clothing store next door. There was a pants outfit in the window and he insisted that I try it on. We went into the store and bought me several outfits. We dated for a while and he took me to his grandson's Bar Mitzvah at one of the hotels. Shortly after, he had a slight heart attack and couldn't see me because he got too excited. He told his family that I wanted too many clothes, which was his cover up. He couldn't tell them that he wanted to have sex with me but it wasn't good for him. I told my friend Sandy the truth and she understood. We let him save face with his family.

I started to work at another hotel and met a nice couple. I asked them if they knew where I could get a leather jacket. The had a single widowed 84-year old brother, whe worked part time at the Merchandise Mart for something to do. The gave me his number and I called him. He invided me to his apartment on the Bay to go out for lunch. After lunch we went back to his place and talked. He was very interesting. He had been a hat manufacturer in New York. He also started the first YMCA. Jimmy Cagney was one the first to join. He used to travel sometimes for his hat firm. He went to Italy to buy felt for his hats. When he was on the road in the Midwest, instead of going home to New York, he went to New Orleans. He knew the madam at an establishment and stayed with her for the weekend. She taught him how to really pleasure a woman. He was one of the brightest men I ever met. I knew if my friends or I had problems we went to him first and he would advise us. Frank had a bar one time and had many interesting stories to tell. The afternoon passed as he asked me to stay for dinner. We went out to eat and came back to his place. I stayed the night and had the best sex ever. He saw that I came several times and he did too. I used to spend weekends with him at his place. He had a masseuse for me every weekend and we ate out. I enjoyed his pool every night as all his friends sat out on the bay. He was very generous with me, he bought me clothes, luggage, handbags, jewelry and whatever I needed or wanted. He also had food connections and bought me steaks and other high quality meats. He had a cleaning woman every day for an hour. When I sold my apartment building and had to wait a month to move into my new one, I stayed with him.

Frank had a married daughter, she and her husband lived about 75 miles north of him. When they came in, we all went out for dinner. He also had a son who was a doctor in Chicago. He would always say "you added an extra 10 years to my father's life". We were good for each other. When he was ill, I looked after him until he was better. But, eventually I broke up with him and moved on.

I bought another small building, 5 units, in Bay Harbor and moved. I didn't like it though because it needed constant repairs. I sold it and bought a condo in Hallandale. When I bought my first building in Bay Harbor, my daughters mother in-law called. She had just lost her husband and her sister was visiting her. They had a dance at her condo and wanted me to go with her sister as she couldn't attend. I said "no" but she talked me into it. I danced a bit and tried to get someone to dance with her sister, but they all refused. We left early to meet my daughter's mother in-law and she was talking to a gentleman and introduced me to him. A month later I met this fellow, Ray, in Surfside Shopping Center. We talked a while and discovered that neither of us liked my daughter mother in-law. He asked me for my phone number and I gave it to him. A week later I got a phone call, he was going to pick me up in an hour and take me to breakfast in his brand new car. I should be ready and hung up. I got dressed and decided to take a chance. He and his father had just sold their lingerie business in New York and made millions and retired. He was divorced and decided to play the stock market quite heavily. We dated several times and he gave me some good stock marked tips. I made several thousand dollars, so I bought him a pretty cigarette lighter. He was an unusual fellow.

He called me and told me to pack for an overnight trip, which I did. He picked me up and we drove about a hundred miles and stopped at a hotel. We had cocktails and lunch and went to the room he had registered for us. We had sex. He was a wham, bang, thank you man type of sex partner so after sex he decided we should go home. He was an interesting fellow but not the greatest lay. I dated him for the stock tips that I got from him for a while. But when I moved from Bay Harbor to Golden Isles, I didn't see him anymore. He was my age or maybe a few years younger. Before I moved to Golden Isles, I looked for another apartment building.

Before I moved to my first building, I met a young fellow who did television commercials. He was very good looking. He asked me for a date and I said, "yes". He said to dress up as he was taking me someplace special. I looked stunning in a gold brocade outfit that I bought so I wore that. He arrived looking nice. He asked me if I could dance and I said "Of course". He said "let's see" and started to dance with me. Then he tried to kiss me but I said "no". I told him to leave and that was that. I didn't go to bed with everyone who asked me or tried to lead me to bed. I recently saw him on a television commercial for a local restaurant.

I was in a bakery one day and the older gentleman in front of me started to talk to me. He said his wife was terminally ill and asked to see me. I said "I don't date married men" (only sometimes). He asked to call me in the future and I said alright. He called me about a month later and wanted to see me. His wife had passed away. We went to dinner at a wonderful seafood restaurant on the water. I ordered fish for him and lobster for me. He wanted to go to a kosher place, but I insisted on this restaurant. We continued to go out, shop, and do other fun things together. He was very creative. He owned a paint factory in Florida and Puerto Rico. I needed paint rollers for my new building and he gave them to me. He wanted to marry me, but you know how I feel about that. I also met another married man who wanted to date me. I said, "No, I give to the needy, not the greedy". He wanted me to look at some paintings he wanted to buy and I said alright. After a while we eventually went to bed. He bought me paintings and other things. He used to like eating my cunt and asked if he could put whipped cream in my vagina and eat it. I said "Okay". It was an unusual sensation.

I was at the Sun Spa in Hollywood and had been to my chiropractor nearby. He cashed a check for me but was short $35. I stopped at his office to get it. He wasn't there, but the podiatrist who shared his office was there. I told him that Lloyd owed me $35, he said he would give it to me and collect from Lloyd. We talked a bit and he asked if he could see me that night at the spa. I said "okay". It was the funniest sex I ever had. He brought a flashlight that he used to examine parts of my body up close. He insisted on using it between my legs. He said I was very clean and he entered me.

When I worked at a land company, while living in Bay Harbor, I met a nice gentleman from Seattle, Washington who had bought some land and was thinking of selling it. I talked him out of it and he asked me out for a date. We went to see Lena Horne and had a wonderful dinner. He was the head of the biggest pension union in the country and traveled to different places to discuss the union affairs. I got letters from him from Hawaii, Alaska, etc. He was married but his wife was very religious, they lived together but did their own thing. He took me to the finest restaurants and always bought me liquor, flowers, etc. He even sent me grapefruits from Texas. He wrote me from all over the world and enclosed money to buy myself flowers, candy and other things. He offered to put in the personnel business in California with my sister. I said, "No". He paid to send me to my sisters place and he would meet me there. Instead when I got there, he called and had me meet him in Silver Springs, Maryland at a hotel there. He was tall and heavy and luckily came after 2 or 3 strokes. He had to go to meetings and gave me money to go shopping. At night we went to dinner and shows. He was very interesting, generous, but a lousy lay. If this man would have gotten into the White House, I would have gone to the Inaugural Ball with him. Eventually I tired of him and broke it off.

After my three years in the first apartment, I discovered that I was used to having sex after 20 years of marriage just as men were entitled to. So I didn't feel guilty about my sexual activities. I soon learned that men had two heads. If the top one wasn't agreeable, the bottom one certainly was.

I'm glad my time was reasonably safe before sexually transmitted diseases became so prevalent. I never worried about getting a disease, never encountered any, kept my vagina clean, ready, willing, and able at the right time.

I also learned that men enjoyed being aroused like women. They enjoyed having their breasts kissed and played with. Also their balls and other parts of their body. They loved having their penis kissed and sucked.

One day it was raining and when it stopped, I went to the store to pick up some items. I parked and got out of the car. There was a huge puddle on the other side. A nice man said "I wish I had a jacket or something to put over that puddle so you could cross". He led me to the left of the puddle allowing me to cross over a smaller one. I thanked him and we proceeded to talk. He worked for Raytheon and was from Cleveland, my hometown. He was down on business and to visit his mother. At night he visited her. He asked to take me out for a late lunch the next day and I said "yes". I gave him my name and phone number. He called the next day and asked me to lunch. We went to an interesting place in the wholesale furniture district. The clientele was mostly homosexuals. The food was excellent and the scene interesting. The next day he took me for a lovely lunch of Shrimp Tempura.

The third day he asked me to a hotel for lunch and I said, "yes". We had lunch and went to the room he had rented afterwards. When I got to the room, I told him to order me a scotch, which he did. After it was delivered, we both undressed. I noticed he only had one ball. He said he was born that way but it didn't interfere with his life. I told him to stand in front of me and I dipped his beautiful penis into my drink and sucked it off. He was thrilled and got into bed after that. Shortly afterwards, he kissed my breasts and everywhere else. He was all over me. Then he inserted his lovely hot penis into my vagina and we both climaxed together. He took me home shortly thereafter as he was leaving the next day. I received a lovely red traveling clock from him that he sent me from the airport.

I worked for another land company when I lived in Bay Harbor. One night after a party my boss brought me home, he asked if he come back the next night with a swimming cap on. He enjoyed sex that way. I said, "okay". He was my boss and whatever made him happy was all right. Occasionally I went out to dinner and had sex with a few land salesman.

I met Clair and Norm when I was selling land in a big store. They didn't buy, but we became good friends. She read cards and he was handy. He prepared my cabinets and my first four unit apartment building, which hid the fact that they were loose from the wall. Everyone admired the paper. I used to take Claire out for lunch. She would read my cards. Norm was trying to get into me behind Claire's back, but I never let him. Claire fixed me up with a couple of men, but nothing worthwhile. I went to bed with one of them.

I had a tenant and his wife from Columbia in my last apartment building. There were a wealthy couple and had a hotel there, but they sold it and came to Florida. They brought beautiful emeralds and rubies with them. Then they became a masseur and a masseuse. She asked me if he brought home women while she worked. I said "no". I really didn't know, but he tried to make a pass at me. I ignored it.

A couple of years later, I was at a spa on the ocean. The lady masseuses weren't very good. I happened to see him since he ran the men's spa. I mentioned to him about the poor lady masseuses, he told me to let him give me a good massage. He was really good. I agreed and had a great massage plus a good lay afterwards. It was a pleasant surprise. I returned to my room and the phone rang. My married friend the mover called. He was supposed to come over at 6 o'clock but was in the neighborhood and was coming over sooner. I quickly showered and put on a gown. He arrived. Another good lay. Two within an hour. It ended up a nice day.

* Before I moved to Golden Isles, I looked for another apartment building in Miami Beach. I saw a sign for a two-family building. I inquired about it. The owner was semi-retired. He bought little buildings and sold them in South Beach. He had an accident and was almost blind.

He could do everything but drive, count money, and a few other things. He asked me out to dinner and we became quite friendly. I learned a lot about real estate for small buildings from him. He was about 10 years older than myself and a good sport. He loved to dress up and go out. In fact, we took a couple of trips to a resort about 200 miles away for a few days. I took him shopping for food and of course, I shopped for myself at the same time. He used to like to grill steaks and was very good with plants. He had orange and grapefruit trees in the yard. He was well built and fair in bed. One night he entered me with his penis and stopped. He said it was nice to know I was there if he wanted me. He also took care of my car and bought me clothes. Sometimes he would buy chickens and I made him chicken soup, which he liked and put in the freezer. He wanted to marry me, but I didn't want to get married. I saw him off and on until I married the second time (that was a big mistake).

My podiatrist's secretray asked me if I wanted to meet a nice man. I said "yes". She told me to call Al who had seen me in th office and wanted to meet me. I said "okay" and called him one day. He invited me over to his condo in Hallandale. He wasn't driving right now as he was waiting for an eye operation. We had a drink, danced, and talked. He was quite charming. He was retired and his parents owned a catering buisiness. He owned bars and restaurants. He had also taught cooking at Pratt Institute. He was an excellent cook and I enjoyed being with him. He was tall, well built and I felt his strenght when I was with him. It was hard for him to maintain an erection though because of his medication but we managed to enjoy sex anyhow with the help of mouths and hands. When he kissed me I almost came in my pants. There was something about him that I found very sexy. That didn't happen to me with other men. One night a neighbor at Al's place asked us over for porno movies. We enjoyed them. When Al was in the hospital, that neighbor took me out for dinner and bed and geve me pieces of jewelry. He wanted to marry me but I daid "no".

I also worked the telephones for a land company. I became friendly with two married fellows I worked with, Marty and Dave. We worked nights and they cmae overduring the day, just to talk. When I moved to Golden Isles they visited me and Betsy, my neighbor, came over to ask if they wanted to see her apartment, one at a time. After they left Betsy told me she gave a blowjob to both of them and made $10 apiece. I was furious at her. I was laid up with a bad leg in bed, so I was stuck with her company I had a nice female tenant in my second building who was a travel agent. She used to join me for Harry's breakfasts. Meanwhile, I got a job as a social director in North Carolina. I went up there and after a few weeks, a waitress introduced me to a widowed gentleman. He took me out of couple of times. Then I found out that my boss had hired some college kids but fired them without paying them at the end of the season. He didn't give me my phone messages from my family nor from the gentleman who took me out. So I quit and called the gentleman to pick me up. He was thrilled. I told him that I was going to sue the owner and he was glad to help me. I stayed with him awhile and then drove north to see my children. When I came back, this fellow wanted to marry me. I said I didn't know him well enough. I stayed with him til a lawsuit came up and then went home. He begged me to marry him, but I said "no". He was fair in bed. He took me to different attractions in the area, flea markets, swimming, water slides, shows and for many good fish dinners.

Marty, who was older than Dave visited me later when I moved to Sunrise. He had a bad marriage and we went to bed a couple of times out of friendship. I also worked customer relations for a land company and after a couple of months my boss asked me over for dinner. By the time I got there he was so drunk I put him to bed, joined him for the night and I don't think we had sex. I left early the next morning.

A couple of weeks after I was home, I got a letter from Sol Allar from New York. He didn't seem to know the woman he was writing. I showed the letter to my neightbor and friend Adrienne. She told me to answer the letter. I did and we started corresponding. I was working at the Marco Polo Hotel as a social director. I liked it there and the hotel owners liked me. Shortly after, they hired a new manager from New York who didn't understand Florida hotels. He wanted me to account for every prize and keep daily records. I quit. The bosses begged me not to, but I couldn't handle the pressure from the manager. Meanwhile Sol invited me to visit him in New York. He sent me the money for a ticket. I went there to meet him. He never had any children and had been widowed for three years. He was a pharmacist and a great golfer. He was tall and well built and also well endowed. He took me to his apartment in the Bronx. It was a nice 3 bedroom apartment with a dog. We went out for dinner and on the way, we stopped at a driving range. He was amazed that I could hit the ball so well. We had dinner and talked.

He had two brothers and at one time his father owned 5 million dollars of real estate in the Bronx. He never told me that. His brother told me later. Sol's pharmacy burned down and he went to work for someone. I stayed in the hotel one night and then moved to his apartment. He had a cute dog that peed on the bed when I slept there. We always had to lock him up in a small room off the kitchen.

Sol had some sexy movies that we watched and then went to bed. I stayed a week or two and then went home. He was very generous to me, he always left money in a drawer, and on weekend we ate out. He bought me new glasses since I had broken mine. He also bought me a pretty orange raincoat and whatever else I wanted or needed. He had some plastic beads which he inserted up his ass during sex and then asked me to pull them out as he came. He enjoyed that. When I got home, he sent me some Hustler and Penthouse Magazines. He ordered some black underwear for me from Frederick's of Hollywood in California. I knew it wouldn't fit so I went to a lingerie store and bought some black hose, a girdle and a black bra. I had holes put in the bra where the nipples were. It looked stunning on me. He was thrilled. He was very religious but very sex oriented. One day I called my old landlord Fred, who was married by now. He picked me up for lunch and a nice roll in the hay at a hotel and gave me money to take a taxi back to Sol's. It was a nice afternoon. Sol took me to look at engagement rings. I went but I knew I wasn't going to marry him. He took me to see his friend, a doctor, to find out why I wouldn't marry him. I told his friend that I like living in Florida better than New York. I thought.....if I really loved him, it wouldn't matter. Anyhow, we broke up but he continued to call until he realized it was hopeless.

When I decided to sell my Golden Isles Apartments, the agent brought a nice man over to look at it. I was in a bathing suit and he seemed to look at me more than the apartment. Anyhow, they left and an hour later the buyer came back to visit me. We talked awhild and decided on a price for the apartment. The phone rang and it was a gentleman friend. I siad to him "are you taking me out to dinner?". He said yes so I said goodbye the other man. Just then, the real estate agent called and said that they couldn't find the buyer, he was supposed to be at their office. I acted as if I didn't anything about his where abouts. As soon I got off the phone with my real estate agent I sent the gentleman over to the real estate office to sign the contract. Later we got all dressed up and he took me to dinner. He was a good looking Italian gentleman with his own plumbing business up north and decided he wanted a little vacation place in Florida. Married, of course. We went to a lovely place for dinner and came home to bed. He was a good lover and we enjoyed the night together. The next morning we had breakfast and went swimming in my pool. That was last I saw of him, he went back home shortly after that night.

Al was a well traveled man who had a married daughter in England who he complained he didn't hear from unless she needed money. He had been a widower for a couple of years. He was a very sexy guy. I could almost come in my pants when he kissed me. He had sugar diabetes that interfered with his lovemaking. But, we enjoyed each other. He was an excellent cook and very handy. He talked me into buying a place in his development that had a nice pool and clubhouse. But then they started to build

I-95 behind me and I decided to move. Which I did, to Hallandale. I sold his place for him when he was in the hospital and he moved to Inverrary, Jackie Gleason's place in Ft. Lauderdale. I continued to see him off and on until I got married again. We liked to shower together and enjoyed sex sometimes in the shower. Both he and Sam were mad when I got married because I married a man I'd known for two weeks. They had wanted to marry me but I'd "No". I got vertigo and met this man named George through my girlfriend Sandy. I had a date with him and he went to New Jersey and started calling and writing. I said what are you looking for, a pen pal, and don't bother me. He sent me a check to come up to Jersey and also buy a suit. I went up there and to see if that helped my vertigo. I went to New Jersey. He wined and dined me, bought me lots of clothes and was very generous. After two weeks, I said I was going home. He told me someone that we were getting married. I called my girlfriend Sandy and my daughter for advice. They both told me to get married. He was 15 years olders than I was and very wealthy. So I married him.

I wanted to leave him after a year, but he talked me out of it. He was a jack rabbit in bed and had trouble satisfying me. Enough of that mistake. Anyhow, both Sam and Al were angry because they both wanted to marry me. Back when I was single in Hallandale, I was still dating Al and Sam. There was a woman in the building who was divorced and turned pro for a while. She had trouble getting money from her ex-husband. It was a small building with mostly Canadian owners who came for the winter only. Betsy came over often. Uninvited, but she was someone to talk to. I had hurt my leg so I wasn't working. She applied for a weekend job with a gentleman baby sitting, so to speak. She didn't get the job. I asked if she would mind if I called him. I got the job. He was a wealthy old man in an oceanfront apartment who was afraid to be alone.

He had a maid who was off on Saturdays and Sundays. I did no housework and just serve and eat with him on weekends. He had a niece in the building who was a wealthy basket case. She was almost childlike. Anyhow, the maid left food for lunch and dinner, but I told her not to because I didn't like cooking. So, I cooked for us. I had my own room and bath and television. Sometimes I played cards with him in the afternoon or he went to the pool. He wanted me to go too but I said I wasn't interested. I daid I would rather nap instead. The pay was excellent for the weekend and I just relaxed there. I could talk to my friends by phone or do anything else I wanted to. During the week, I dated either Sam of Al. My girlfriend Sandy fixed me up with a man that she met at the nutrition center. I went to dinner with him then went home.

When I bought my apartment in Sunrise, the owner's brother lived there. A nice Italian family. He painted the apartment for me. I say this because we went to church affairs with them after I married the second time. Meanwhile, when I moved in, the brother-in-law Frank came over frequently. He picked up new shades for the porch, painted my dining room set, and of course, took me to bed. I knew his wife and it was embarassing. He was attracted to me. In fact he noticed clothes that the other boyfriends had bought me and insisted on giving me money to buy a dress from him. He used to take his wife and me shopping and managed to be at my place a lot with some excuse or another. He was a quick lay, and not a good one at that, but it made him happy. He did all the fixing and chauffeuring for me. When I married the second time, my new husband and I went to church dances with them.

My husband died after 18 years of marriage. The first man I had after that was his best friend who we both knew for 20 years. We lived in the same building at one time. He suggested playing gin with me as he did my husband. I said fine. He came over and we played. When we went to leave, he tried to kiss me. I resisted at first and thought what the hell. So I kissed him and before you knew it we were in bed. I dipped his penis in scotch and sucked it, which he enjoyed and we had sex. He took me out to dinner for birthday but he wasn't for me.

The next one was a gentleman in my building who lost his girlfriend and was interested in me. He hadn't had sex for many years. The first time we had sex he slept for 12 hours completely worn out. He was in his 80's. The next time he went home and had to do oxygen. The third time he really enjoyed himself.

I was swimming one day when a married man much younger than myself started to flirt with me. One day he was at the pool without his wife and told me to go home and leave my door unlocked. I was still getting out of my bathing suit when he took his off in the dining room and came into the bedroom where I was. We kissed, he sucked my breasts, ate my cunt, then entered me all in 10 minutes. It was nice but too fast for me. No more of him.

The names of the people in my book are fictitious or deceased. Also, my memory in not 100% accurate after all these years.

The names of the people in my book are fictitious or deceased. Also, my memory in not 100% accurate after all these years.

I'm fortunate to be able to say I've had a full and happy life and if I had to do it it again, I wouldn't change anything. I might add a few things, Like...........I would love to meet **Oprah Winfrey** *whom I admire greatly and consider one of the brightest people in the world. Also, I would like to meet* **Bill Clinton,** *whom I consider the sexiest man alive. But until then, I'm resting waiting to see what the future holds. Maybe a nice, older, wealthy gentleman for dating. I may be old but I'm still very much* **ALIVE.**

With Grandma the Sexpot, you don't need viagra.

Good-bye for now

Made in the USA
Middletown, DE
30 January 2022